D0913176

Sports Illustrated KIDS

A SUPERFAN'S GUIDE TO

PRO Hockey TEAMS

▶▶▶▶▶▶▶▶▶▶

By Tyler Omoth

CAPSTONE PRESS
a capstone imprint

Sports Illustrated Kids Pro Teams Sports Guides are published by Capstone Press, a Capstone Imprint, 1710 Roe Crest Drive, North Mankato, Minnesota 56003. www.capstonepub.com

Library of Congress Cataloging-in-Publication Data is available on the Library of Congress website

ISBN: 978-1-5157-8843-0 (library binding)
ISBN: 978-1-5157-8855-3 (eBook PDF)

Editorial Credits

Elizabeth Johnson and Nate LeBoutillier, editors; Terri Poburka, designer; Eric Gohl, media research; Gene Bentdahl, production specialist

Photo Credits

Dreamstime: Jenta Wong, 42r, Jerry Coli, 3l, 10l, 11r, 36r, 45r, 56r; Getty Images: Bruce Bennett, 8l, 29r, 32l, 60l, Denis Brodeur, 58l; Newscom: Cal Sport Media/Aaron Doster, 23l, 43l, Cal Sport Media/Anthony Nesmith, cover (bottom), Cal Sport Media/Billy Hurst, 54r, Cal Sport Media/Del Mecum, 22r, 30r, Cal Sport Media/Joe Camporeale, 21l, Cal Sport Media/Manny Flores, 24r, 25l, Cal Sport Media/Mike Langish, 40r, Icon SMI/Adam Davis, 20r, Icon SMI/IHA, 18l, 20l, Icon SMI/Richard C. Lewis, 30l, Icon SMI/TSN, 55r, Icon Sportswire/Bob Frid, 60r, Icon Sportswire/Danny Murphy, 39l, Icon Sportswire/Fred Kfoury III, 12r, 13l, Icon Sportswire/Nick Wosika, 65l, USA Today Sports/John E. Sokolowski, 59l, USA Today Sports/Perry Nelson, 29l, ZUMA Press/Jeff Mcintosh, 31l, ZUMA Press/Jeff Wheeler, 34r, ZUMA Press/Joel Marklund, 14r, 16r, ZUMA Press/Nathan Denette, 58r, ZUMA Press/Sean Kilpatrick, 46r; Shutterstock: cover (top), Abel Tumik, throughout (puck), Alexander Ishchenko, throughout (stick), Chones, throughout (trophies), Kyle Besler, 26r, Luca Santilli, 68–69bkg, 70–71bkg, 72, Mega Pixel, throughout (pennant), Pavel Hlystov, throughout (skates); Sports Illustrated: Bob Rosato, 31r, 56l, 59r, 62l, Damian Strohmeyer, 40l, 44r, 47l, 47r, 57r, 64l, 70bl, David E. Klutho, 2l, 2r, 3m, 6l, 7r, 8r, 9l, 9r, 10r, 11l, 14l, 15l, 15r, 17l, 17r, 19l, 19r, 21r, 22l, 23r, 24l, 25r, 27l, 28r, 33r, 34l, 35l, 35r, 37l, 38l, 38r, 39r, 41l, 45l, 46l, 48r, 49l, 50r, 51r, 52l, 53l, 53r, 54l, 55l, 57r, 61r, 63r, 69b, 70t, 70br, Hy Peskin, 4–5, 37r, 69t, John Biever, 26l, John D. Hanlon, 48l, John G. Zimmerman, 68, John Iacono, 43r, John W. McDonough, 2m, 18r, Manny Millan, 28l, 41r, Richard Meek, 27r, Robert Beck, 3r, 6r, 7l, 32r, 33l, 52r, 61l, 62r, 65r, Simon Bruty, 51l, 63l, 64r, Tony Triolo, 16l, 36l, 44l, 49r, 50l, Walter Iooss Jr., 12l, 13r, 42l

Design Elements: Shutterstock

All statistics are calculated through the 2016–17 NHL regular season.

Printed in Canada
010395F17

TABLE OF CONTENTS

FOLLOW EVERY TEAM

Ask a Stars fan who scored the goal that gave the franchise its only Stanley Cup, and he'll tell you it was Brett Hull. Ask an Oilers fan who notched 50 goals in just 39 games, and she'll tell you it was Wayne Gretzky. Ask a Devils fan what position Martin Brodeur played, and he'll tell you Brodeur was a goalie who broke many records.

Hockey fans are devoted to their favorite teams. They know all the players' names and faces. They have memorized the crucial dates and important records in their favorite team's history. And they're loyal through bad times, always feeling sure things will be different next year. That's what it means to be a fan.

It's something else to be a superfan. What's the difference? Superfans want to know it all. They steep themselves in the stories and numbers that tell the story of National Hockey League (NHL). They check the results of every game and track the standings all season long. They follow every team. They can't get enough.

Anaheim
DUCKS

The Anaheim Ducks first took the ice in 1993 as the Mighty Ducks of Anaheim. They were originally owned by the Walt Disney Company. The team was sold in 2005, and the new regime changed the name to the Anaheim Ducks before the 2006–07 season. The Ducks won their only Stanley Cup trophy that same year.

OVERALL RECORD
(WINS-LOSSES-TIES-OVERTIME LOSSES):
865-709-107-139

HOME ICE:
Honda Center

SUPERFACT

The Mighty Ducks of Anaheim was originally a tip-of-the-hat to the Disney movie series, *The Mighty Ducks*. They were the only team in major North American sports to be named after a movie franchise.

Then & Now

TEEMU SELANNE 1996–2001; 2005–14 / JAKOB SILFVERBERG 2013–present

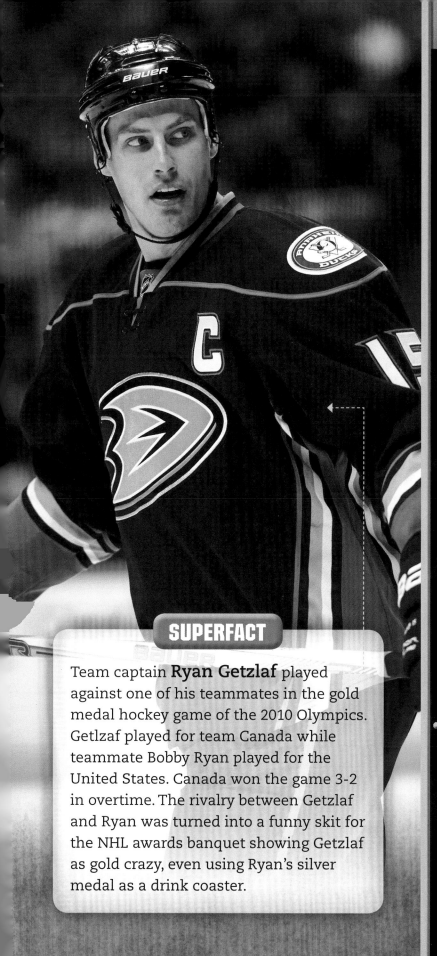

Championships:
2007

Franchise Leaders
- *Games:* **Teemu Selanne, 966**
- *Goals:* **Teemu Selanne, 457**
- *Points:* **Teemu Selanne, 988**
- *Assists:* **Ryan Getzlaf, 578***
- *Hat Tricks:* **Teemu Selanne, 13**
- *Saves:* **Guy Hebert, 11,813**

SUPERFACT

Team captain **Ryan Getzlaf** played against one of his teammates in the gold medal hockey game of the 2010 Olympics. Getlzaf played for team Canada while teammate Bobby Ryan played for the United States. Canada won the game 3-2 in overtime. The rivalry between Getzlaf and Ryan was turned into a funny skit for the NHL awards banquet showing Getzlaf as gold crazy, even using Ryan's silver medal as a drink coaster.

Arizona COYOTES

The Arizona Coyotes got their start in the World Hockey Association (WHA) as the Winnipeg Jets in 1972. When the WHA was disbanded in 1979, the Jets became part of the NHL. The team moved to Arizona in 1996 and became the Phoenix Coyotes. In 2014 they became the Arizona Coyotes.

OVERALL RECORD:
1,210-1,337-266-131

HOME ICE:
Gila River Arena

SUPERFACT

In 1989 the Coyotes retired jersey number 9 in honor of the great Bobby Hull. When the team signed his son, Brett, in 2004, the team un-retired the jersey number so Brett could wear it while playing for the Coyotes.

Then & Now
BOBBY HULL 1972–80 / RADIM VRBATA 2016–present

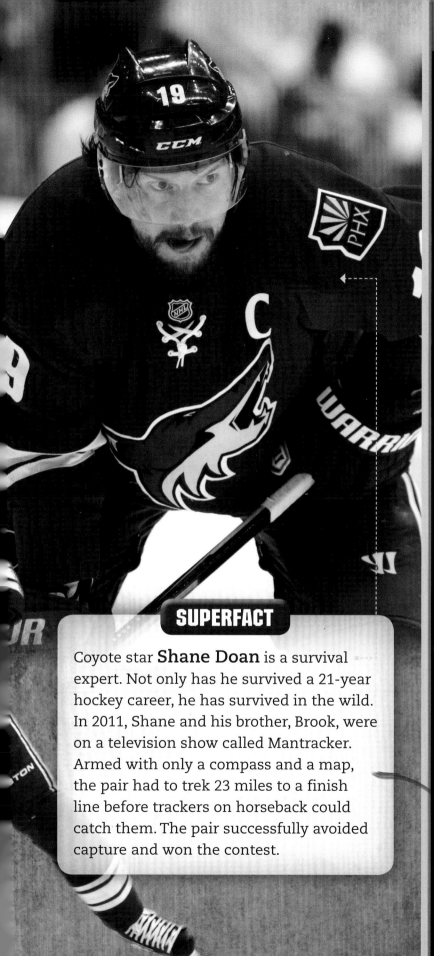

SUPERFACT

Coyote star **Shane Doan** is a survival expert. Not only has he survived a 21-year hockey career, he has survived in the wild. In 2011, Shane and his brother, Brook, were on a television show called Mantracker. Armed with only a compass and a map, the pair had to trek 23 miles to a finish line before trackers on horseback could catch them. The pair successfully avoided capture and won the contest.

TROPHY CASE

Championships:
None

Franchise Leaders
Games: Shane Doan, 1,540
Goals: Shane Doan, 402
Points: Shane Doan, 972
Shutouts: Mike Smith, 22
Hat Tricks: Keith Tkachuk, 9
Saves: Mike Smith, 8,763

Boston
BRUINS

The Boston Bruins were the first United States hockey team to join the NHL. The previously all-Canadian league welcomed the Bruins in 1924. Since then, the Bruins have been one of the most successful teams in the league. Boston most recently won the Stanley Cup after the 2010–11 season.

OVERALL RECORD:
3,065-2,329-791-151

HOME ICE:
TD Garden

SUPERFACT

The Bruins original owner, Charles Adams, was also the owner of the First National grocery store chain. The chain's colors were brown and yellow. Adams chose to use those colors for the Bruins, as well for marketing purposes. The colors later changed to today's black and gold.

Then & Now
PHIL ESPOSITO 1967–75 / ZDENO CHARA 2006–present

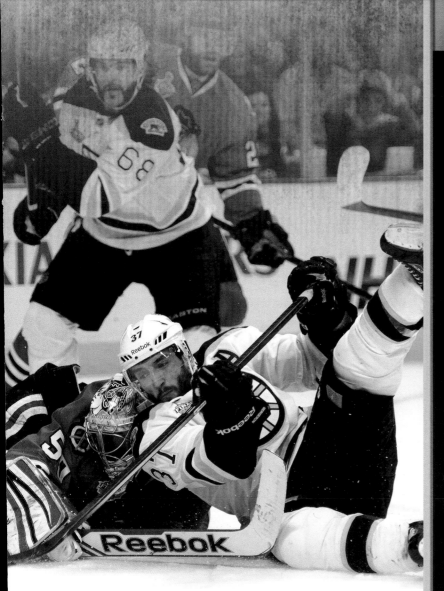

Championships:
  1929, 1939, 1941, 1970, 1972, 2011

Franchise Leaders:
  Games: **Ray Bourque, 1,518**
  Goals: **John Bucyk, 545**
  Points: **Ray Bourque, 1,506**
  Plus/Minus: Bobby Orr, +589
  Hat Tricks: **Cam Neely, 13**
  Saves: **Tim Thomas, 10,533**

SUPERFACT

When the Bruins won the Stanley Cup in 2011, **Patrice Bergeron** became a member of the Triple Gold Club. The Triple Gold Club is an honorary title for players who have won an Olympic Gold Medal, a World Championship, and a Stanley Cup. He is the only player in Bruins history to join the club.

Buffalo
SABRES

The Buffalo Sabres joined the NHL before the 1970–71 season as an expansion franchise. While the team has made it to the playoffs 29 times, even competing in the Stanley Cup Finals twice, they have never won a championship.

OVERALL RECORD:
1,702-1,415-409-130

HOME ICE:
KeyBank Center

SUPERFACT

From 2007 to 2010, the Sabres had a logo that depicted a portion of a bison leaping forward. The yellow, oddly curved logo garnered the nickname, "The Buffaslug."

Then & Now
JIM LORENTZ 1972–78 / JACK EICHEL 2015–present

TROPHY CASE

Championships:
None

Franchise Leaders
- *Games:* **Gilbert Perreault, 1,191**
- *Goals:* **Gilbert Perreault, 512**
- *Points:* **Gilbert Perreault, 1,326**
- *Assists:* **Gilbert Perreault, 814**
- *Hat Tricks:* **Alexander Mogilny, 10**
- *Saves:* **Ryan Miller, 14,847**

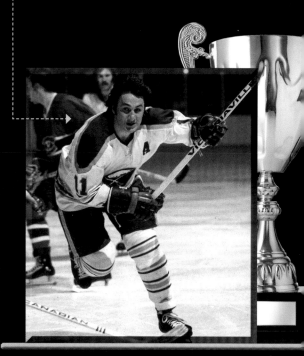

SUPERFACT

Sabres right wing man, **Brian Gionta**, was raised near Rochester, New York. At 5-foot-7, he is one of the shortest players in the NHL. Because he's small, but very fast on the ice, the local media refers to him as the "Rochester Rocket." In the offseason, Gionta rockets back home and works in his father's hardware store.

Calgary FLAMES

The Flames first played as an NHL franchise in 1972 in Atlanta. The team owner chose the nickname Flames in recognition of the fires that destroyed parts of Atlanta during the Civil War. The team was sold in 1980 and moved to Calgary, Alberta, Canada. The team kept the nickname despite the move. The Flames won the Stanley Cup in 1989.

OVERALL RECORD:
1,616-1,382-379-123

HOME ICE:
Scotiabank Saddledome

SUPERFACT

By rule, all NHL hockey jerseys must be secured during play by a "fight strap." In February 2017, Flames forward Kris Versteeg was ejected after a fight because his opponent was able to pull his jersey off.

Then & Now
JAROME IGINLA 1996–2013 / MIKAEL BACKLUND 2008–present

Flames captain **Mark Giordano** lost his sister in a car accident in 1998 and still thinks about her during the national anthem. When the song is over, he taps his stick on his helmet twice in silent tribute to her.

TROPHY CASE

Championships:
1989

Franchise Leaders
Games: **Jarome Iginla, 1,219**
Goals: **Jarome Iginla, 525**
Points: **Jarome Iginla, 1,095**
Assists: **Al MacInnis, 609**
Hat Tricks: **Theoren Fleury, 13**
Saves: **Miikka Kiprusoff, 14,631**

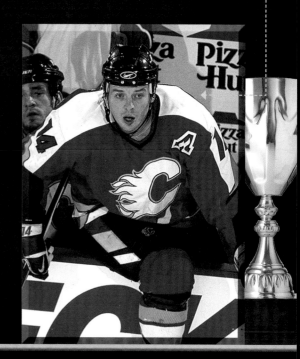

Carolina
HURRICANES

The Carolina Hurricanes originated as the New England Whalers, playing their games in Boston in 1971. The team moved to Hartford, Connecticut, before the 1974–75 season. They were a part of the WHA from 1971 to 1979 but joined the NHL when the two leagues merged in 1979. In 1997 the team moved once again, this time to North Carolina, becoming the Carolina Hurricanes.

OVERALL RECORD:
1,205-1,333-263-143

HOME ICE:
PNC Arena

SUPERFACT

Even though the Carolina team is nicknamed the Hurricanes, their team mascot is a pig. "Stormy" the pig is a tribute to the successful pork industry in North Carolina, and a mainstay at Hurricane games and events.

Then & Now
GORDIE HOWE 1977–80 / VICTOR RASK 2014–present

Championships:
2006

Franchise Leaders
Games: **Ron Francis, 1,186**
Goals: **Ron Francis, 382**
Points: **Ron Francis, 1,175**
Assists: **Ron Francis, 793**
Hat Tricks: **Eric Staal, 13**
Saves: **Cam Ward, 16,186**

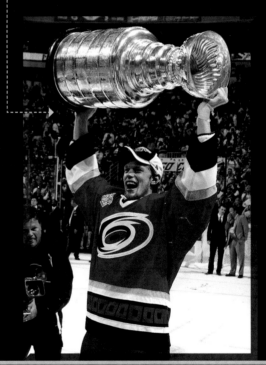

SUPERFACT

Hurricanes winger **Jeff Skinner** is a great skater. In fact, he won a bronze medal at the 2004 Canadian Junior National Figure Skating Championships. He claims that the techniques he learned in figure skating helped his hockey game. In recent years other NHL hockey players have hired figure skaters to help them improve their skating.

Chicago
BLACKHAWKS

The Chicago Blackhawks were one of the first teams to join the NHL in the United States. They officially joined the league in 1926 along with two other U.S.-based teams. Since their beginning, the Blackhawks have been one of the most successful teams on the ice. They've made the playoffs 61 times and have won six Stanley Cups.

OVERALL RECORD:
2,687-2,633-814-136

HOME ICE:
United Center

SUPERFACT

Frederic McLaughlin founded Chicago's pro hockey team and named it in honor of his military unit. McLaughlin served as a commander of the 333rd Machine-Gun Battalion of the 86th Division of the U.S. Army, otherwise known as the Blackhawks.

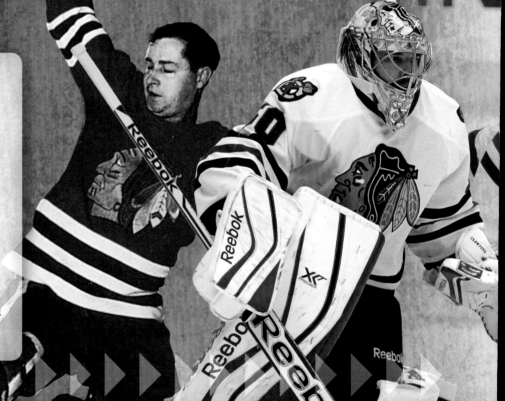

Then & Now
GLENN HALL 1957–67 / COREY CRAWFORD 2005–present

Championships:
1934, 1938, 1961, 2010, 2013, 2015

Franchise Leaders

Games: **Stan Mikita, 1,394**

Goals: **Bobby Hull, 604**

Points: **Stan Mikita, 1,467**

Assists: **Stan Mikita, 926**

Saves: **Ed Belfour, 9,763**

Youngest to score Stanley Cup OT goal: **Patrick Kane (2010)**

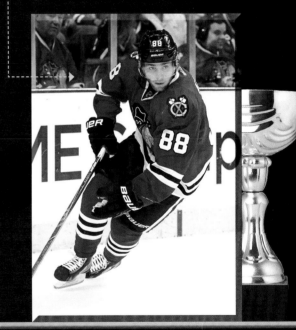

SUPERFACT

After helping the Blackhawks win the Stanley Cup in 2010, team captain **Jonathan Toews** won the Conn Smythe Trophy for the Stanley Cup Playoff MVP. His hometown of Winnipeg, Manitoba, Canada was so proud of him that city officials named a lake after him. Today, residents can learn to skate on a lake named after their hometown hero.

Colorado
AVALANCHE

The Colorado Avalanche first existed as a WHA team named the Quebec Nordiques. The Nordiques franchise was awarded to owners in San Francisco but moved to Quebec before its first season. After some initial success, the team struggled for a long stretch and finally moved to Colorado as the Avalanche in 1995. Since then the Avalanche have brought home two Stanley Cup trophies.

OVERALL RECORD:
1,342-1,234-261-107

HOME ICE:
Pepsi Center

SUPERFACT

In 2011 the Avalanche retired jersey number 77 in honor of the great Ray Bourque. Oddly enough, Bourque played only a little more than one season with the Avalanche, but he did help them win the Stanley Cup in 2001.

Then & Now

RAY BOURQUE 2000-01 / GABRIEL LANDESKOG 2011-present

Budding superstar **Nathan MacKinnon** has talents beyond just hockey. In 2014 he was a guest star on the Canadian TV show, Mr. D. The show highlights the adventures of a high school teacher. MacKinnon played a student who is in detention for missing too many classes. His character was playing hooky to play hockey.

TROPHY CASE

Championships:
  1996, 2001

Franchise Leaders
  Games: **Joe Sakic, 1,378**
  Goals: **Joe Sakic, 625**
  Points: **Joe Sakic, 1,641**
  Assists: **Joe Sakic, 1,016**
  Hat Tricks: **Joe Sakic, 15**
  Saves: **Patrick Roy, 11,924**

Columbus Blue
JACKETS

The Columbus Blue Jackets joined the NHL in 2000 as an expansion franchise. It's been tough on the ice for the Blue Jackets in their 16 years. They've only made the playoffs twice during that time. With several consecutive winning seasons in recent years, however, the Blue Jackets look to become a mainstay in the playoffs for years to come.

OVERALL RECORD:
535-589-33-121

HOME ICE:
Nationwide Arena

SUPERFACT

The Blue Jackets are named to honor the patriots from Ohio that fought in the Civil War. A replica cannon is fired during home games when the Blue Jackets take the ice, score a goal, or win a game.

Then & Now
ADAM FOOTE 2005–08 / ALEXANDER WENNBERG 2014–present

Current Blue Jackets star **Cam Atkinson** helped a young girl get a dog. Maddie Wright went to a game on her ninth birthday. Her parents told her if the player she picked scored a goal, they could get a dog. She picked Cam and it was a good choice. He scored and a few weeks later they brought "Cam" the dog to meet Cam the Blue Jacket.

TROPHY CASE

Championships:
None

Franchise Leaders
- *Games:* **Rick Nash, 674**
- *Goals:* **Rick Nash, 289**
- *Points:* **Rick Nash, 547**
- *Assists:* **Rick Nash, 258**
- *Hat Tricks:* **Rick Nash, 5**
- *Saves:* **Marc Denis, 7,251**

Dallas STARS

The Dallas Stars originally entered the NHL in 1967 as the Minnesota North Stars. The team played in Minnesota from 1967 to 1993. Though the team found success in Minnesota, they moved to Dallas in 1993. They were an immediate success, making the playoffs seven of their first eight seasons in their new home. They won the Stanley Cup in 1999.

OVERALL RECORD:
1,697-1,601-459-125

HOME ICE:
American Airlines Center

SUPERFACT

The Stars introduced a new mascot, Victor E. Green, for the 2014–15 season. Victor, known as "Vic," is a fuzzy green alien with hockey sticks for antennae.

Then & Now
MIKE MODANO 1989–2010 / TYLER SEGUIN 2013–present

SUPERFACT

Jamie Benn is the soft-spoken captain of the Stars. He grew up playing hockey with his brother, Jordie Benn, in Canada. Jamie and Jordie played in Dallas together until late in the 2016–17 season, when Jordie was traded to the Montreal Canadiens. They are one of 15 sets of brothers currently playing in the NHL.

TROPHY CASE

Championships:
1999

Franchise Leaders
Games: **Mike Modano, 1,459**
Goals: **Mike Modano, 557**
Points: **Mike Modano, 1,359**
Assists: **Mike Modano, 802**
Hat Tricks: **Mike Modano, 7**
Saves: **Marty Turco, 11,420**

Detroit
RED WINGS

The Detroit Red Wings are one of the oldest teams in the NHL. They joined the league as the Detroit Cougars in 1926. New ownership changed the name to the Detroit Falcons in 1930. After another buyout the team changed names again in 1932, this time to the Detroit Red Wings. Not only are the Red Wings one of the oldest teams in the NHL, they are one of the most successful with 11 Stanley Cup Championships.

OVERALL RECORD:
2,891-2,419-815-145

HOME ICE:
Little Caesars Arena

SUPERFACT

James Norris bought the Detroit franchise in 1932. He renamed them the Red Wings as a tribute to a team he used to play for called the Montreal Winged Wheelers. He put a car tire into the logo to represent Detroit's famous auto industry.

Then & Now
STEVE YZERMAN 1983–2006 / GUSTAV NYQUIST 2011–present

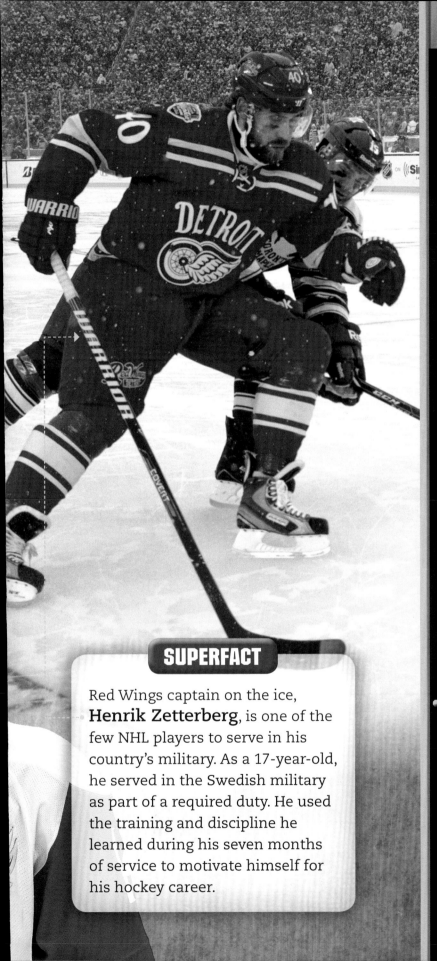

SUPERFACT

Red Wings captain on the ice, **Henrik Zetterberg**, is one of the few NHL players to serve in his country's military. As a 17-year-old, he served in the Swedish military as part of a required duty. He used the training and discipline he learned during his seven months of service to motivate himself for his hockey career.

TROPHY CASE

Championships:
 1936, 1937, 1943, 1950, 1952, 1954, 1955, 1997, 1998, 2002, 2008

Franchise Leaders:
 Games: **Gordie Howe, 1,687**
 Goals: **Gordie Howe, 786**
 Points: **Gordie Howe, 1,809**
 Assists: **Steve Yzerman, 1,063**
 Hat Tricks: **Steve Yzerman, 16**
 Saves: **Chris Osgood, 12,801**

LINDSAY AND HOWE
RED-HOT RED WINGS

Edmonton OILERS

The Alberta Oilers were one of the original 12 teams of the World Hockey Association, playing their first season in 1972–73. The name was changed from Alberta to Edmonton the next season, and the Oilers were eventually absorbed into the NHL in 1979 after the WHA folded. The team, along with its newly acquired young superstar, Wayne Gretzky, quickly found success, winning five Stanley Cup Championships in their first 11 seasons in the league.

OVERALL RECORD:
1,326-1,215-262-141

HOME ICE:
Rogers Place

SUPERFACT

When the Oilers acquired 17-year-old Watne Gretzky, they gave him jersey number 99. He wore it well. Today, the number 99 is retired across the NHL in honor of "The Great One."

Then & Now
WAYNE GRETZKY 1978–88 / RYAN NUGENT-HOPKINS 2011–present

SUPERFACT

Oilers captain **Connor McDavid** began skating before he was three years old. By the time he was a young teenager, he was already a budding hockey superstar. To practice his coordination and skating he created an obstacle course in his family's driveway using items like paint cans and hockey sticks. He wouldn't let himself hang out with his friends until he ran through his drills each day.

TROPHY CASE

Championships:
1984, 1985, 1987, 1988, 1990

Franchise Leaders
Games: Kevin Lowe, 1,037
Goals: **Wayne Gretzky, 583**
Points: **Wayne Gretzky, 1,669**
Assists: **Wayne Gretzky, 1,086**
Game-Winning Goals: **Glenn Anderson, 72**
Saves: **Bill Ranford, 11,508**

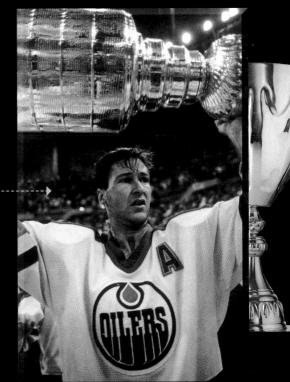

Florida PANTHERS

The Florida Panthers joined the NHL in 1993 as an expansion franchise. The Panthers quickly found success, playing in the Stanley Cup Final just three seasons later. Success in the following years was hard to come by for the Miami-based team. Hope is on the way with two recent Rookie of the Year winners: Jonathan Huberdeau in 2012–13 and Aaron Ekblad in 2014–15.

OVERALL RECORD:
737-768-142-173

HOME ICE:
BB&T Center

SUPERFACT

In 2016 the Florida Panthers changed their uniforms and logo. They ditched the previous logo of a leaping panther in favor of a shield emblem with a panther head on it. The new image represents a more serious and dedicated team image.

Then & Now
OLLI JOKINEN 2000–08 / JAROMIR JAGR 2015–present

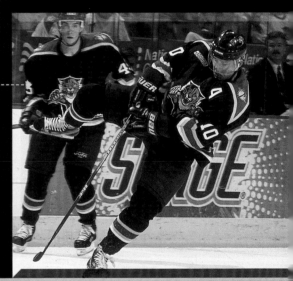

SUPERFACT

When Panthers goalie **Roberto Luongo** was a kid, he loved hockey, but wasn't a very good skater. His parents wanted him to play forward and work on his skating skills. One day when he was 11-years-old, his team's goalie didn't show up. Luongo begged to fill in at the position and had a shutout. Today he's one of the best goalies in the NHL.

Los Angeles
KINGS

The Los Angeles Kings took the ice in 1967 as an expansion team in the NHL. The team found immediate success, reaching the playoffs each of its first two seasons. The Kings have made it to the playoffs 29 times in 49 years, bringing home the Stanley Cup twice. The great Wayne Gretzky played some of his best hockey during his years with the L.A. Kings.

OVERALL RECORD:
1,628-1,695-424-135

HOME ICE:
Staples Center

SUPERFACT

The L.A. Kings have had a wide variety of jersey colors. The original uniforms featured purple and yellow. In 1988 they switched to black and silver. Then in 1998 they added purple to the silver and black.

Then & Now

TIGER WILLIAMS 1985–87 / DREW DOUGHTY 2008–present

TROPHY CASE

Championships:
2012, 2014

Franchise Leaders
Games: **Dave Taylor, 1,111**
Goals: **Luc Robitaille, 557**
Points: **Marcel Dionne, 1,307**
Assists: **Marcel Dionne, 757**
Hat Tricks: **Luc Robitaille, 13**
Saves: Jonathan Quick, **11,806**

SUPERFACT

L.A. Kings star forward **Anze Kopitar** was born in Jesenice, Slovenia. His family moved to the United States in 2006 when he was drafted by the Kings. No matter where he lives, he knows how to communicate. Kopitar speaks five languages including English, Swedish, German, Serbian, and Slovene. He is the only Slovenian to win a Stanley Cup.

Minnesota WILD

After the North Stars left in 1993, Minnesota hockey fans didn't have an NHL team to cheer on for seven years. Finally Minnesota was granted a new team for the 2000-01 season: the Wild. The Wild have had moderate success, but have not made it all the way to the Stanley Cup Finals yet. With a strong fan base, the Wild look to build a winning team again in the Land of 10,000 Lakes.

OVERALL RECORD:
607-494-55-122

HOME ICE:
Xcel Energy Center

SUPERFACT

The Wild logo shows the head of a wild animal with a forest background. The eye of the animal is a star, a tribute to Minnesota's former NHL team, the North Stars, that departed in 1993.

Then & Now

NIKLAS BACKSTROM 2006–15 / DEVAN DUBNYK 2015–present

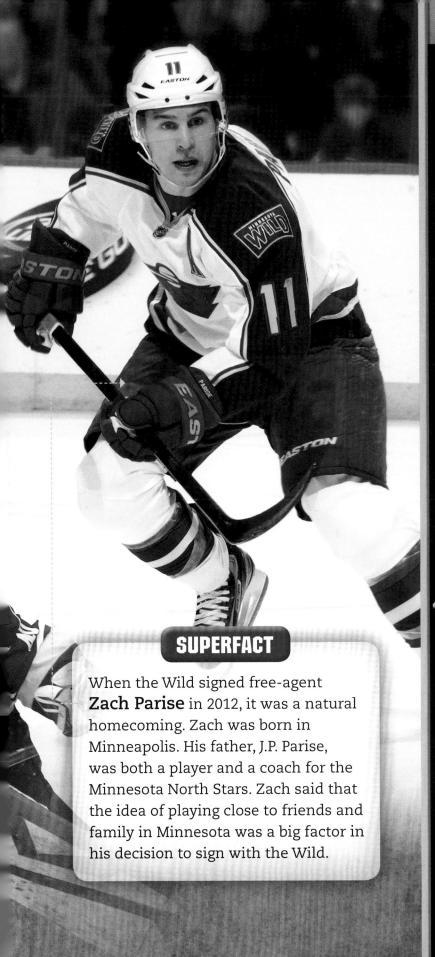

TROPHY CASE

Championships:
None

Franchise Leaders
Games: **Mikko Koivu, 843**
Goals: **Marian Gaborik, 219**
Points: **Mikko Koivu, 614**
Assists: **Mikko Koivu, 435**
Hat Tricks: **Marian Gaborik, 9**
Saves: **Niklas Backstrom, 10,321**

Montreal
CANADIENS

Founded in 1909, the Montreal Canadiens are the longest continuously operating professional hockey team in the world. They are also the only NHL team that existed before the NHL itself. When it comes to championships, the Canadiens have been the most successful franchise in pro hockey history.

OVERALL RECORD:
3,345-2,180-837-134

HOME ICE:
Bell Centre

SUPERFACT

Many people refer to the Canadiens simply as the Habs. It is short for Les Habitants, a name given to French settlers in the Montreal area.

Then & Now
GUY LAFLUER 1971–85 / MAX PACIORETTY 2008–present

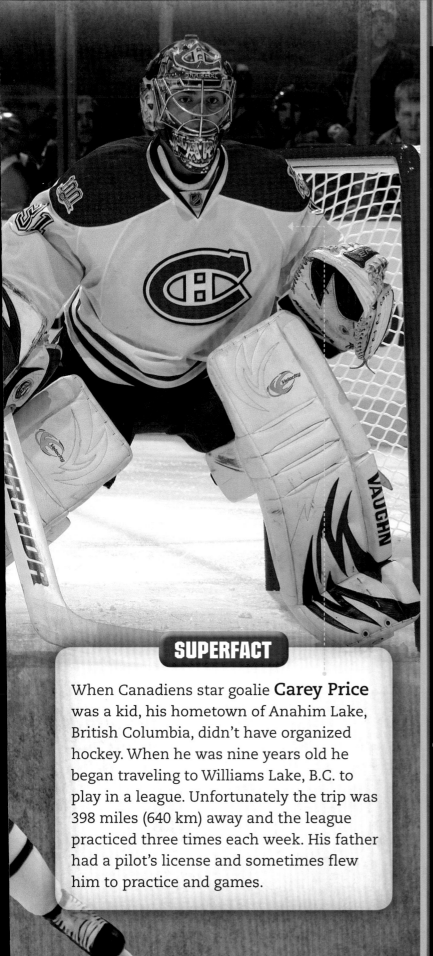

SUPERFACT

When Canadiens star goalie **Carey Price** was a kid, his hometown of Anahim Lake, British Columbia, didn't have organized hockey. When he was nine years old he began traveling to Williams Lake, B.C. to play in a league. Unfortunately the trip was 398 miles (640 km) away and the league practiced three times each week. His father had a pilot's license and sometimes flew him to practice and games.

TROPHY CASE

Championships:
1916, 1919, 1924, 1925, 1930, 1931, 1944, 1946, 1953, 1956, 1957, 1958, 1959, 1960, 1965, 1966, 1968, 1969, 1971, 1973, 1976, 1977, 1978, 1979, 1986, 1993

Franchise Leaders
Games: Henri Richard, **1,256**

Goals: Maurice Richard, **544**

Points: **Guy Lafleur, 1,246**

Assists: **Guy Lafleur, 728**

Wins: **Jacques Plante, 314**

Saves: **Patrick Roy, 13,883**

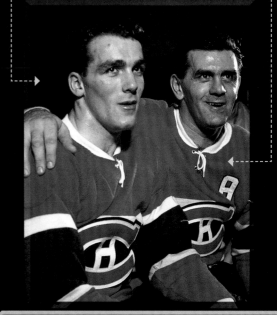

Nashville
PREDATORS

The Nashville Predators played their first season in 1998–99 as an NHL expansion franchise. After 18 seasons, the Predators finally made it to the Stanley Cup Finals. They have been a consistently good team on the ice for years. They've had only six losing seasons in franchise history. The name Predators was suggested by former owner Craig Leipold.

OVERALL RECORD:
686-560-60-136

HOME ICE:
Bridgestone Arena

SUPERFACT

In 1971 an excavation in downtown Nashville uncovered the bones of a saber-toothed tiger. In honor of that discovery, the Nashville Predators depict a saber-toothed tiger on their logo.

Then & Now

JORDIN TOOTOO 2003–12 / MIKE FISHER 2011–present

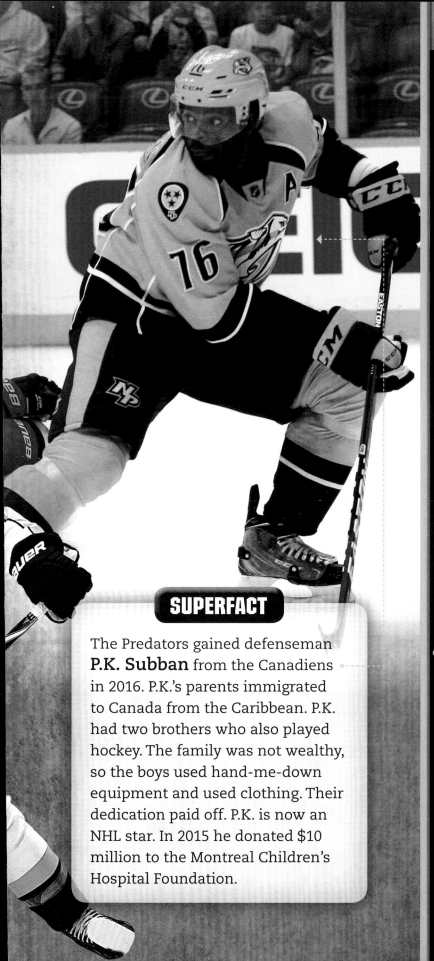

SUPERFACT

The Predators gained defenseman **P.K. Subban** from the Canadiens in 2016. P.K.'s parents immigrated to Canada from the Caribbean. P.K. had two brothers who also played hockey. The family was not wealthy, so the boys used hand-me-down equipment and used clothing. Their dedication paid off. P.K. is now an NHL star. In 2015 he donated $10 million to the Montreal Children's Hospital Foundation.

TROPHY CASE

Championships:
  None

Franchise Leaders
  Games: **David Legwand, 956**
  Goals: **David Legwand, 210**
  Points: **David Legwand, 566**
  Assists: **David Legwand, 356**
  Hat Tricks: **Filip Forsberg and Steve Sullivan, 4**
  • *Saves:* **Pekka Rinne, 12,969**

New Jersey DEVILS

The New Jersey Devils got their start as the Kansas City Scouts in 1974. After two years of instability and poor attendance, the team moved to Colorado as the Colorado Rockies. In 1982 the team moved once again, this time to New Jersey. They were renamed the New Jersey Devils. Since their move to the East Coast, the Devils have been consistent contenders in championship runs and have won three Stanley Cups.

OVERALL RECORD:
1,412-1,473-328-131

HOME ICE:
Prudential Center

SUPERFACT

The Jersey Devils got their nickname from a legendary creature that is rumored to live in the Pine Barrens forest in New Jersey. Reports of the fearsome creature date back as far as the 1700s. The creature has yet to be captured.

Then & Now

SCOTT NIEDERMAYER 1991–2004 / DAMON SEVERSON 2014–present

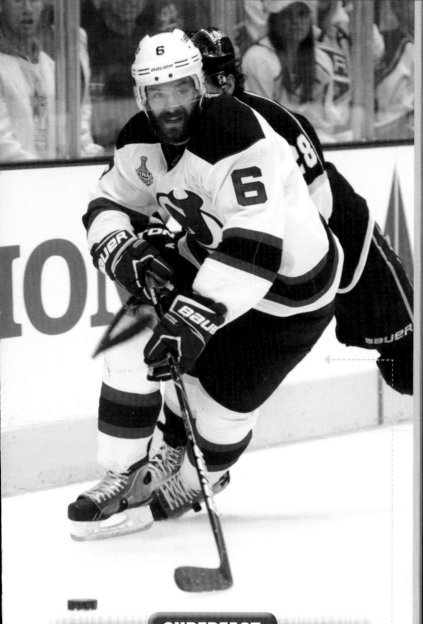

TROPHY CASE

Championships:
1995, 2000, 2003

Franchise Leaders
- *Games:* Ken Daneyko, 1,283
- *Goals:* Patrik Elias, 408
- *Points:* Patrik Elias, 1,025
- *Assists:* Patrik Elias, 617
- *Hat Tricks:* Patrick Elias, 8
- *Saves:* Martin Brodeur, 28,776

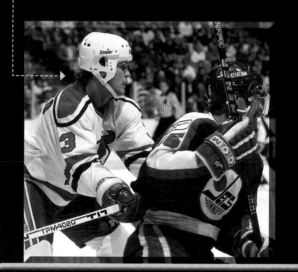

SUPERFACT

When Devils defenseman **Andy Greene** graduated college, he went undrafted by the NHL. He had his degree in education and thought about becoming a physical education teacher. The New Jersey Devils didn't draft him, but they did contact him and offer him a contract. It was a good move. For a player who was considered too small and too slow to draft, Andy Greene has become the team captain and a fan favorite.

New York ISLANDERS

The New York Islanders joined the NHL in 1972 as an expansion team. Despite New York already having a team within the city (the New York Rangers), the NHL granted a franchise to ownership in Long Island. In 2015 the team moved their home games to Brooklyn, but kept the same name. The Islanders have had moderate success since their creation. For a brief span from 1979 to 1983, the Islanders ruled the NHL, winning the Stanley Cup championship four years in a row.

OVERALL RECORD:
1,538-1,483-347-132

HOME ICE:
Barclays Center

SUPERFACT

Sparky the Dragon served as a mascot to the New York Dragons arena league football team. When the Islanders moved into the same arena, they adopted Sparky as their own. He was retired briefly in 2015, but was brought back by popular demand.

Then & Now
DENIS POTVIN 1973–88 / JOHN TAVARES 2009–present

Championships:
  1980, 1981, 1982, 1983

Franchise Leaders
- *Games:* **Bryan Trottier, 1,123**
  Goals: **Mike Bossy, 573**
  Points: **Bryan Trottier, 1,353**
  Assists: **Bryan Trottier, 853**
  Hat Tricks: **Pierre Turgeon, 8**
  Saves: **Rick DiPietro, 8,044**

SUPERFACT

Islanders right wing **Cal Clutterbuck** is more than just a great player on the ice. He's the team DJ. Clutterbuck picks out the pregame music in the locker room as well as the team's warm-up songs. He'll play a little bit of something for everyone, including rock, hip-hop, and rap. When a player likes a new song, they let him know and he'll add it to the list for the next game.

New York
RANGERS

The New York Rangers started out early and with great success. The team joined the NHL in 1926. They had a winning first season and won the Stanley Cup in their second season on the ice. Over their 90 seasons the Rangers have made the playoffs 58 times and won the Stanley Cup Championship four times, most recently in 1993–94.

OVERALL RECORD:
2,753-2,590-808-119

HOME ICE:
Madison Square Garden

SUPERFACT

On February 3, 2009 the Rangers retired jersey number 9 in honor of Adam Graves. On February 22, 2009, they retired number 9 again, this time to recognize former Ranger great, Andy Bathgate.

Then & Now
JOHN DAVIDSON 1975–83 / RYAN MCDONAGH 2010–present

SUPERFACT

Rangers goalie **Henrik Lundqvist** is one of the NHL's best between the pipes. When he's not on the ice, he likes to keep it cool by playing guitar. In fact, when he played hockey for the Frolunda Indians in Sweden, he and some teammates started a band called Box Play. They wore big black wigs and rocked out. Today Lundqvist still plays the guitar and sometimes takes the stage with bands he knows.

TROPHY CASE

Championships:
1928, 1933, 1940, 1994

Franchise Leaders
Games: **Harry Howell**, 1,160
Goals: **Rod Gilbert**, 406
Points: **Rod Gilbert**, 1,021
Assists: **Brian Leetch**, 741
Saves: **Henrik Lundqvist**, 19,307
Hat Tricks:
Mark Messier and **Petr Nedved**, 6

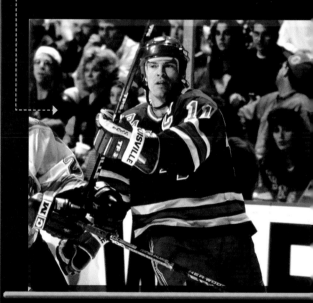

Ottawa
SENATORS

The Ottawa Senators played their first game as an NHL expansion franchise in 1992. The team was named the Senators after a team that had previously existed in Ottawa, but left for St. Louis in 1934. Since the reincarnation of the team, they have been consistent competitors in the playoffs, reaching them 15 out of 24 seasons. Despite many trips to the playoffs, the Senators have yet to win a Stanley Cup Championship.

OVERALL RECORD:
866-788-115-135

HOME ICE:
Canadian Tire Centre

SUPERFACT

Winger Bobby Ryan decided to change his jersey number. He announced the change from 6 to 9 via Twitter video, playing Drake's song "9." The lyrics say "turn the 6 upside down, it's a 9 now."

Then & Now

JASON SPEZZA 2002–14 / BOBBY RYAN 2013–present

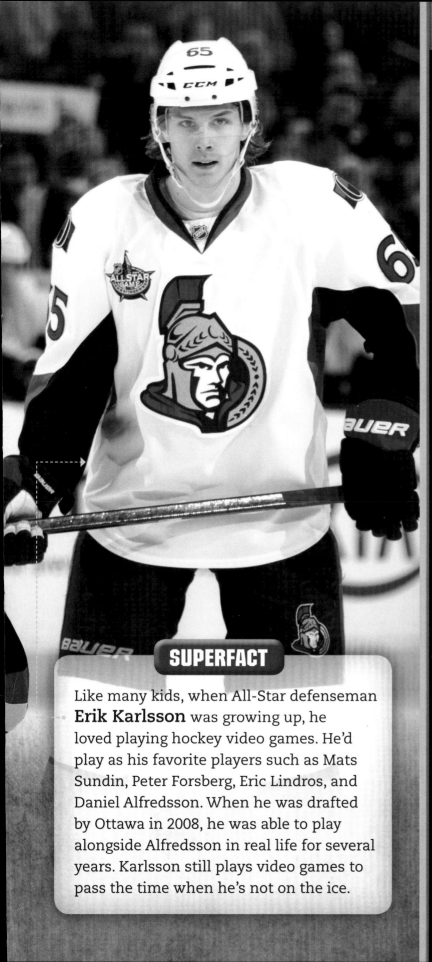

SUPERFACT

Like many kids, when All-Star defenseman **Erik Karlsson** was growing up, he loved playing hockey video games. He'd play as his favorite players such as Mats Sundin, Peter Forsberg, Eric Lindros, and Daniel Alfredsson. When he was drafted by Ottawa in 2008, he was able to play alongside Alfredsson in real life for several years. Karlsson still plays video games to pass the time when he's not on the ice.

TROPHY CASE

Championships:
None

Franchise Leaders
Games: **Chris Phillips, 1,179**
Goals: **Daniel Alfredsson, 426**
Points: **Daniel Alfredsson, 1,108**
Assists: **Daniel Alfredsson, 682**
Hat Tricks: **Daniel Aflredsson, 8**
Saves: **Craig Anderson, 8,428**

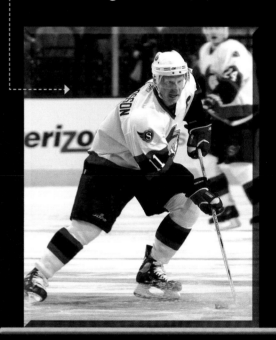

Philadelphia
FLYERS

The Philadelphia Flyers joined the NHL in 1967 as a new expansion team. It didn't take long for them to win over Philadelphia hockey fans and win on the ice. They reached the playoffs each of their first two years and won the Stanley Cup Final in both the 1973–74 and 1974–75 seasons. The Flyers have not won the Cup again since, but they have been one of the NHL's most consistent teams, making the playoffs in 38 of their 49 seasons.

OVERALL RECORD:
1,934-1,345-457-146

HOME ICE:
Wells Fargo Center

SUPERFACT

When Philadelphia was granted a franchise in 1967, team owners held a "name the team" contest. More than 100 people sent in "Flyers." The team randomly selected one person to win the grand prize, a nine-year-old boy named Alec Stockard.

Then & Now
BOBBY CLARKE 1969–84 / WAYNE SIMMONDS 2012–present

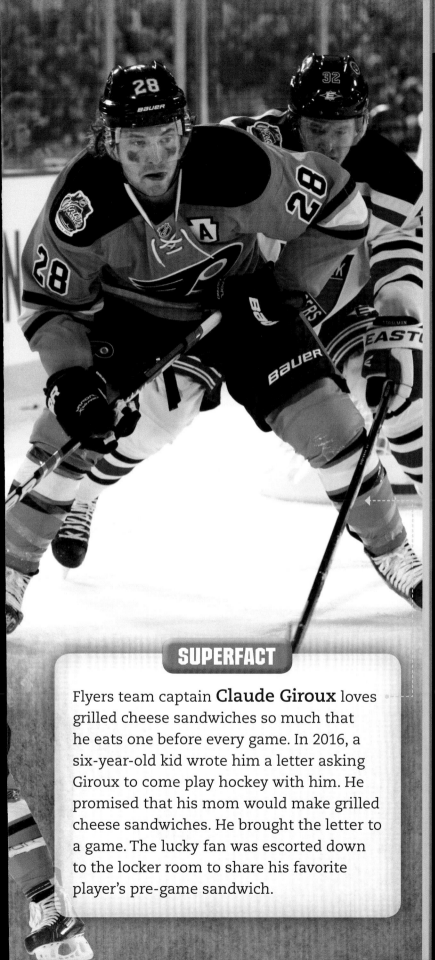

SUPERFACT

Flyers team captain **Claude Giroux** loves grilled cheese sandwiches so much that he eats one before every game. In 2016, a six-year-old kid wrote him a letter asking Giroux to come play hockey with him. He promised that his mom would make grilled cheese sandwiches. He brought the letter to a game. The lucky fan was escorted down to the locker room to share his favorite player's pre-game sandwich.

TROPHY CASE

Championships:
1974, 1975

Franchise Leaders
Games: **Bobby Clarke, 1,144**

Goals: **Bill Barber, 420**

Points: **Bobby Clarke, 1,210**

Assists: **Bobby Clarke, 852**

Saves: **Ron Hextall, 11,669**

Single-season penalty minutes: **Dave Schultz, 472 (1974–75)**

Pittsburgh
PENGUINS

The Pittsburgh Penguins were a part of the first NHL expansion, when the league went from from 6 to 12 teams in 1967. In 49 seasons the Penguins have built a rich history with great players like Mario Lemieux, Jaromir Jagr, and current superstar Sidney Crosby.

OVERALL RECORD:
1,735-1,640-383-124

HOME ICE:
PPG Paints Arena

SUPERFACT

Sidney Crosby is popular. He's so popular that his number 87 Penguins jersey was the number one selling jersey at the official shop of the NHL for the 2016 season.

Then & Now
GARY INNESS 1973–76 / EVENGI MALKIN 2006–present

TROPHY CASE

Championships:
  1991, 1992, 2009, 2016

Franchise Leaders
  Games: **Mario Lemieux, 915**
  Goals: **Mario Lemieux, 690**
  Points: **Mario Lemieux, 1,723**
  Assists: **Mario Lemieux, 1,033**
  Hat Tricks: **Mario Lemieux, 33**
  Saves: **Marc-Andre Fleury, 17,774**

SUPERFACT

Practice makes perfect, and Penguins superstar **Sidney Crosby** practiced his shooting a lot as a kid. While growing up he would shoot pucks into his parents' clothes dryer. Even as good as he was, he missed plenty of shots. The dryer kept working but was riddled with dings and dents that were the battle scars of young Crosby's training. Today the dryer is an honored exhibit at the Nova Scotia Sports Hall of Fame.

51

San Jose
SHARKS

The San Jose Sharks brought NHL hockey to the Bay area of California in 1991. It didn't take long for the team to become a consistently competitive force in the Western Conference. The Sharks reached the playoffs in just their third season on the ice. They reached the Stanley Cup final in 2015–16, but came up short against the Pittsburgh Penguins.

OVERALL RECORD:
929-802-121-132

HOME ICE:
SAP Center

SUPERFACT

The Sharks know how to make an entrance. They lower a 17-foot shark mouth that serves as a tunnel. The lights go down and the team skates out of the shark's mouth and onto the ice while the speakers blast music.

Then & Now

SCOTT HANNAN 1998–2007; 2013–15 / JOE PAVELSKI 2006–present

TROPHY CASE

Championships:
None

Franchise Leaders
Games: **Patrick Marleau, 1,493**
Goals: **Patrick Marleau, 508**
Points: **Patrick Marleau, 1,082**
Assists: **Joe Thornton, 722**
Hat Tricks: **Jonathan Cheechoo, 9**
Saves: **Evgeni Nabokov, 13,463**

SUPERFACT

Logan Couture is an all-star center for the San Jose Sharks, but he'd love to be between the pipes. As a kid he loved playing goalie in neighborhood hockey games. Though he's never played the position in organized leagues, he sits in on goalie meetings with the Sharks. He even begs the coaches to let him play the position in practice.

St. Louis
BLUES

The St. Louis Blues joined the NHL when the league expanded from 6 teams to 12 in 1967. Remarkably the Blues made it to the Stanley Cup Finals in each of their first three seasons. The team has yet to win it all despite reaching the playoffs in 40 of their first 49 seasons.

OVERALL RECORD:
1,771-1,546-432-133

HOME ICE:
Scottrade Center

SUPERFACT

In 2015 the Blues Instagram account mistakenly said "roar bacon" instead of "roar back" when describing a comeback by the team. Fans embraced the mistake, and team captain David Backes put a Blues T-shirt on a pig and dubbed him Piggy Smalls, a new team mascot.

Then & Now
AL MACINNIS 1994–2004 / JADEN SCHWARTZ 2011–present

SUPERFACT

Blues superstar **Vladimir Tarasenko** has a few tricks up his sleeve. At the Kontinental Hockey League's (a Russian league) Skills Competition in 2012, he raced towards the net and goaltender with a puck. He flipped the puck out in front the goaltender, but when the goalie chased it, Tarasenko pulled it back and then shot it in. He'd had the puck attached to his stick with fishing line. Even the goalie laughed.

TROPHY CASE

Championships:
None

Franchise Leaders
Games: **Bernie Federko, 927**
Goals: Brett Hull, **527**
Points: **Bernie Federko, 1,073**
Assists: **Bernie Federko, 721**
Hat Tricks: **Brett Hull, 27**
Saves: **Curtis Joseph, 7,940**

Tampa Bay
LIGHTNING

The Tampa Bay Lightning stormed into the NHL in 1992. The franchise got off to a slow start, making the playoffs just once in its first decade on the ice. But in 2003–04 they made up for it by winning the Stanley Cup Finals. Led by captain Steven Stamkos, the Lighting made another run at the Cup in 2014–15, but lost to the Chicago Blackhawks in six games.

OVERALL RECORD:
790-870-112-132

HOME ICE:
Amalie Arena

SUPERFACT

The Lightning use the image of a lightning bolt as a part of their logo. Because of the image, many fans refer to the Lightning as "the Bolts."

Then & Now
MARTIN ST. LOUIS 2000–14 / VICTOR HEDMAN 2009–present

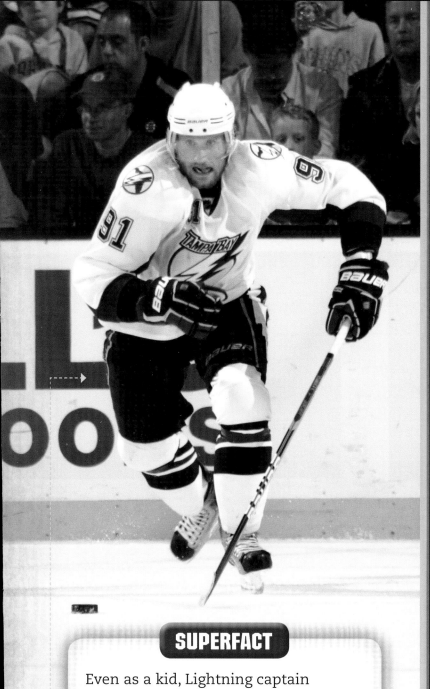

Championships:
- 2004

Franchise Leaders

Games: **Vincent Lecavalier, 1,037**

Goals: **Vincent Lecavalier, 383**

Points: **Martin St. Louis, 953**

Assists: **Martin St. Louis, 588**

Hat Tricks: **Martin St. Louis and Steven Stamkos, 8**

Saves: **Ben Bishop, 5,728**

SUPERFACT

Even as a kid, Lightning captain **Steven Stamkos** wanted to shoot the puck like the NHL greats he watched on TV. Stamkos learned by practicing – a lot. He sometimes shot as many as 500 pucks in a day. It worked. Today Stamkos is one of the best goal scorers in the game. His signature shot is the one-timer, a shot made by hitting the puck as it is passed to him without controlling it first.

Toronto
MAPLE LEAFS

The Toronto Maple Leafs are one of the oldest teams in the NHL. They got their start as the Toronto Arenas in 1917. They didn't waste any time. They won the NHL Finals in 1917–18. They switched to the Toronto St. Patricks from 1919 to 1926. In 1927, new ownership changed the name once again, this time to the Maple Leafs. The Maple Leafs have won 13 Stanley Cups over their long and storied history.

OVERALL RECORD:
2,834-2,736-783-143

HOME ICE:
Air Canada Centre

SUPERFACT

When the NHL declared that teams must have player names on their jerseys in 1977, Toronto's owner didn't like it. The Maple Leafs jerseys had the names stitched in blue on the blue jerseys, making them impossible to read.

Then & Now

DARRYL SITTLER 1970–82 / JAMES VAN RIEMSDYK 2012–present

TROPHY CASE

Championships:
1918, 1922, 1932, 1942, 1945, 1947, 1948, 1949, 1951, 1962, 1963, 1964, 1967

Franchise Leaders
Games: **George Armstrong, 1,187**
Goals: **Mats Sundin, 420**
Points: **Mats Sundin, 987**
Assists: **Borje Salming, 620**
Hat Tricks: **Wendel Clark, 6**
Saves: **Felix Potvin, 10,107**

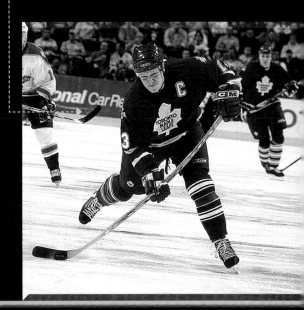

SUPERFACT

Leafs center **Auston Matthews** was the number one overall draft pick in the 2016 NHL draft, so he's truly a gifted hockey player. As a kid, though, hockey may not have been his best sport. The exceptional hand-eye coordination that makes him such a good puck handler also made him a great hitter in baseball. In the end, hockey was his passion and the Maple Leafs can be thankful for that.

Vancouver CANUCKS

The Canucks became the first NHL team in Vancouver, Canada, when they joined the league in 1970. Vancouver had previously had a pro team named the Millionaires. They also had a minor league team called the Canucks, which the NHL franchise adopted. While the Canucks have made their share of playoff appearances, they have yet to win a Stanley Cup.

OVERALL RECORD:
1,524-1,614-391-127

HOME ICE:
Rogers Arena

SUPERFACT

What is a Canuck? The term Canuck is a nickname for Canadians that originated as far back as the mid-1800s. While some find the name offensive, the Vancouver hockey team embraced it.

Then & Now

TIGER WILLIAMS 1980–84 / BO HORVAT 2014–present

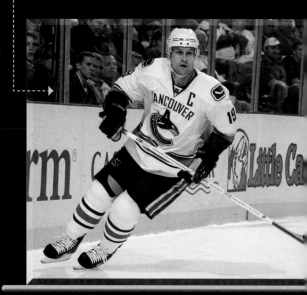

TROPHY CASE

Championships:
None

Franchise Leaders
Games: **Hendrik Sedin, 1,248**
Goals: **Daniel Sedin, 370**
Points: **Henrik Sedin, 1,021**
Assists: **Henrik Sedin, 784**
Hat Tricks: **Markus Naslund, 10**
Saves: **Kirk McLean 12,801**

SUPERFACT

Canucks star center **Henrik Sedin** likes playing on the same team as his twin brother, **Daniel Sedin**. As they grew up, they always played on the same team, even as pros in European leagues. When they entered the NHL draft, the Canucks made a trade to get an extra draft pick and selected both brothers with successive picks. Today the twin Sedin brothers are two of the best players on the Canucks' roster.

Washington
CAPITALS

The Washington Capitals took the ice for the first time at the start of the 1974–75 NHL season. After struggling for the team's first eight seasons, the Caps put together their first winning season in 1982–83 and then reached the playoffs for 14 consecutive years. While the Capitals have never won the Stanley Cup, they're a consistent force in the NHL led by team captain Alex Ovechkin.

OVERALL RECORD:
1,526-1,380-303-135

HOME ICE:
Verizon Center

SUPERFACT

Capitals team captain Alex Ovechkin wears the number 8 on his jersey to honor his mother. His mom, Tatyana Ovechkin, was a point guard for the 1976 and 1980 Russian Olympic women's basketball teams.

Then & Now

JAROMIR JAGR 2001–04 / NICKLAS BACKSTROM 2007–present

TROPHY CASE

Championships:
None

Franchise Leaders
Games: **Calle Johansson, 983**
Goals: **Alex Ovechkin, 558**
Points: **Alex Ovechkin, 1,035**
Assists: **Nicklas Backstrom, 540**
Hat Tricks: Peter Bondra, **19**
Saves: **Olaf Kolzig, 18,013**

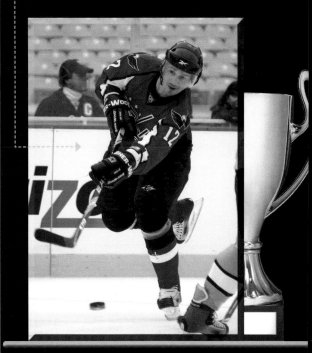

SUPERFACT

Alex Ovechkin skates and plays hockey with style. Off the ice, though, he takes his style a little less seriously. Known for wearing sweatpants to everything, even TV interviews, former teammate Troy Brouwer said that he "has the worst style ever." Brouwer also pointed out that Ovechkin sometimes wears a tuxedo T-shirt underneath his suit coats.

Winnipeg JETS

The Winnipeg Jets got their start as the Atlanta Thrashers in 1999. After 11 seasons of poor play and dwindling fan support, the Thrashers relocated to Winnipeg, Manitoba, Canada. They were renamed the Jets in honor of a previous professional hockey team that had called Winnipeg home from 1972 to 1996.

OVERALL RECORD:
558-628-45-129

HOME ICE:
MTS Centre

SUPERFACT

For playoff games and other big games, Winnipeg fans know just what to wear. They all wear their white Jets T-shirts, jerseys, and sweatshirts to create the "Winnipeg Whiteout." The stands become a sea of white in support of the home team.

Then & Now

MARIAN HOSSA 2005–08 / TOBY ENSTROM 2007–present

SUPERFACT

Jets captain **Blake Wheeler** may be a star on the ice, but that doesn't mean his teammates are afraid to prank him. When Wheeler and his wife bought a new home, his Jets teammates put up a sign on the house that had a picture of Blake playing hockey and read "Knock for a free autograph." It didn't take long for at least one fan to notice and knock on his door.

TROPHY CASE

Championships:
None

Franchise Leaders
Games: **Chris Thorburn, 709**
Goals: Ilya Kovalchuk, **328**
Points: **Ilya Kovalchuk, 615**
Assists: **Ilya Kovalchuck, 287**
Hat Tricks: **Ilya Kovalchuck, 11**
Saves: **Ondrej Pavelec, 9,961**

MAPPING THE GAME

Edmonton Oilers

Calgary Flames

Winnipeg Jets

Vancouver Canucks

San Jose Sharks

Colorado Avalanche

Los Angeles Kings

Anaheim Ducks

Arizona Coyotes

Dallas Stars

Minnesota
Wild

Montreal
Canadiens

Ottawa
Senators

Boston Bruins

Toronto
Maple Leafs

New York Islanders

New York Rangers

Buffalo
Sabres

Detroit Red
Wings

New Jersey Devils

Chicago
Blackhawks

Columbus
Blue Jackets

Pittsburgh
Penguins

Philadelphia Flyers

Washington Capitals

St. Louis
Blues

Carolina
Hurricanes

Nashville
Predators

Tampa Bay Lightning

Florida Panthers

HOCKEY TRIVIA

ALL-TIME HOCKEY

1. **Which player has scored the most goals in NHL history?**
   A: Sidney Crosby
   B: Brett Hull
   C: Wayne Gretzky
   D: Gordie Howe

2. **Which NHL team has won the most Stanley Cups?**
   A. Chicago Blackhawks
   B. Montreal Canadiens
   C. Boston Bruins
   D. New York Rangers

3. **Which NHL goalie has won the most games?**
   A. Patrick Roy
   B. Roberto Luongo
   C. Ben Bishop
   D. Martin Brodeur

4. **What is the most goals scored in a single season by an NHL player?**
   A. 92
   B. 65
   C. 99
   D. 72

5. **What is the most goals scored by one NHL team in a single game?**
   A. 9
   B. 16
   C. 22
   D. 14

All-Time Hockey Answers:
1:C (894 goals); 2:B (24 times); 3:D (691); 4:A (Wayne Gretzky, 1981–82 season); 5:B (Montreal Canadiens, 3/3/1920)

HOCKEY EQUIPMENT

1. **Who was the first goalie to wear a mask?**
   A. Clint Benedict
   B. Jacques Plante
   C. Patrick Roy
   D. Andy Brown

2. **In what decade did the curved hockey stick blade evolve?**
   A. 1940s
   B. 1950s
   C. 1960s
   D. 1970s

3. **What are material is used to make NHL hockey pucks?**
   A. Hard plastic
   B. Neoprene
   C. Leather
   D. Vulcanized Rubber

4. **Which kind of ice skate has a curved blade?**
   A. Hockey skates
   B. Figure (or recreational) skates
   C. Neither
   D. Both

5. **What year did composite sticks first appear in the NHL?**
   A. 1994
   B. 1988
   C. 1986
   D. 1996

Hockey Equipment Answers:
1:A (1930); 2:C (Bobby Hull and Stan Mikita popularized it); 3:D; 4:D; (though hockey skates have a sharper curve); 5:A

ALL-TIME PRO HOCKEY RECORDS

MOST CAREER REGULAR SEASON GOALS

1. Wayne Gretzky, 894
2. Gordie Howe, 801
3. Jaromir Jagr, 765
4. Brett Hull, 741
5. Marcel Dionne, 731

MOST CAREER PLAYOFF GOALS

1. Wayne Gretzky, 122
2. Mark Messier, 109
3. Jari Kurri, 106
4. Brett Hull, 103
5. Glenn Anderson, 93

MOST HAT TRICKS

1. Wayne Gretzky, 50
2. Mario Lemieux, 40
3. Mike Bossy, 39
4. Brett Hull, 33
5. Phil Esposito, 32

ACTIVE GOALS LEADERS (THROUGH 2016-17)

1. Jaromir Jagr, 765
2. Jarome Iginla, 625
3. Alex Ovechkin, 558
4. Marian Hossa, 525
5. Patrick Marleau, 508
6. Rick Nash, 416
7. Shane Doan, 402
8. Marian Gaborik, 396
9. Joe Thornton, 384
10. Sidney Crosby, 382

READ MORE

Frederick, Shane. *Hockey's Record Breakers.* North Mankato, Minn.: Capstone Press, 2017.

Frederick, Shane. *Six Degrees of Sidney Crosby: Connecting Hockey Stars.* North Mankato, Minn.: Capstone Press, 2015.

Zweig, Eric. *Greatest Goalies.* Hockey Hall of Fame Kids. Richmond Hill, Ontario, Can.: Firefly Books, 2014.

INTERNET SITES

Use FactHound to find Internet sites related to this book.

Visit www.facthound.com

Just type in 9781515788430 and go.

INDEX